That's Good, That's Bad

Jaap Tuinman

CONSULTANTS
Anna Cresswell
Gail Heald-Taylor
Lynda Hodson
Glen Huser

ADVISER
Moira McKenzie

PROGRAMME EDITOR
Kathleen Doyle

Schofield & Sims Ltd
Educational Publishers

Journeys

Level Four
That's Good, That's Bad

© Copyright 1984 by Ginn Canada,
a Division of Xerox Canada Inc.

TEACHER CONTRIBUTORS

Kaye Hipper
Terry Bowers
JoAnne O'Gorman
Sheila Wittie
Jan Stevens

ISBN 0-7217-0551-0

Printed and bound in England
ABCDEFGHIJ 9876543210
First printed 1984

ACKNOWLEDGEMENTS

For kind permission to reprint copyrighted material, acknowledgement is hereby made to the following:

Little, Brown and Company for the play "Chicken Forgets". Adapted from *Chicken Forgets* by Miska Miles; illustrated by Jim Arnosky. Text copyright © 1976 by Miska Miles. Reprinted by permission of Little, Brown and Company in association with The Atlantic Monthly Press.

Peguis Publishers Ltd. for two verses of the poem "There Are Trolls" by John F. Green. Reprinted by permission of Peguis Publishers Ltd.

Frederick Warne (Publishers) Ltd. for the illustrations by Beatrix Potter used in the selection, "Meet Beatrix Potter". Reproduced by permission of Frederick Warne (Publishers) Ltd.

David Higham Associates Limited for the first four lines of "Once Upon a Time" from *The Children's Bells* by Eleanor Farjeon. Published by Oxford University Press.

Contents

Wheels

Wheels go fast,
Wheels go slow,
Wheels go round,
Go, wheels, go.

Have You Seen Wheels?

By Lou Arrell
Illustrated by Pauline McGraw

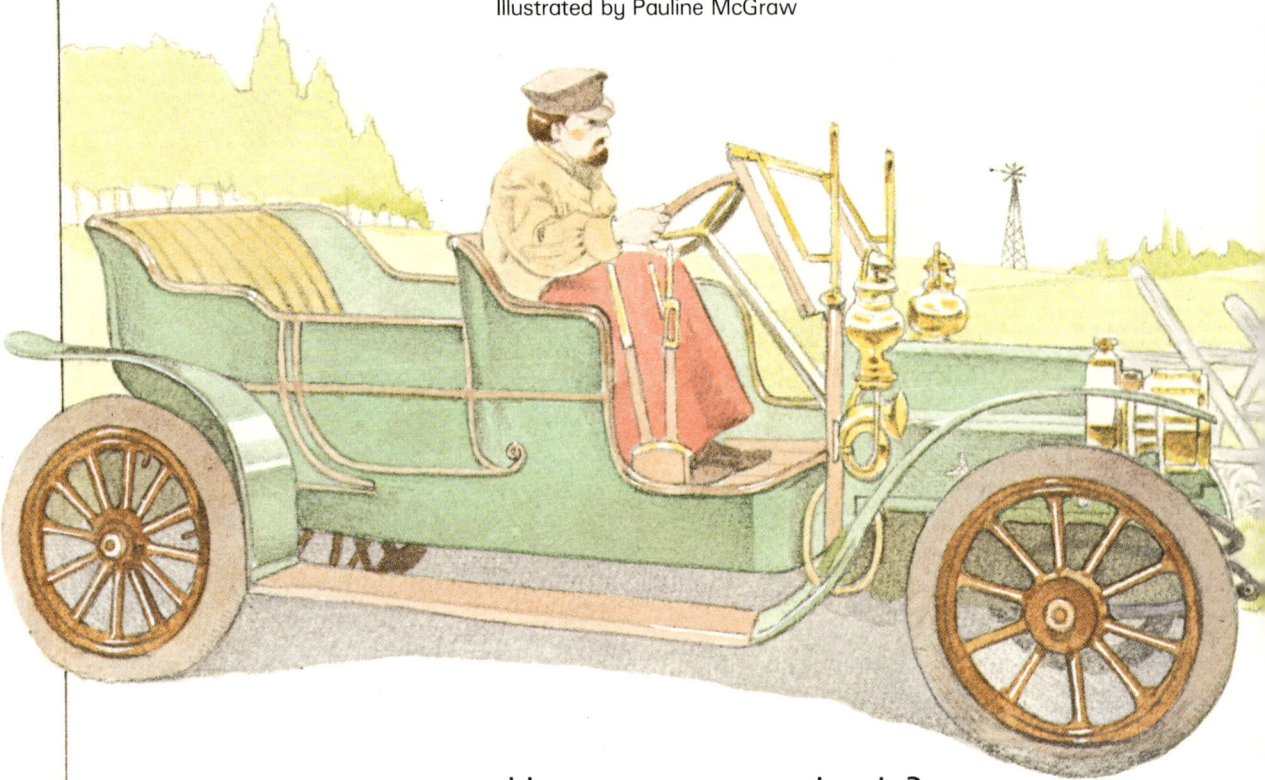

Have you seen wheels?
Fast wheels,
Slow wheels,
Moving,
Rolling,
Turning wheels.

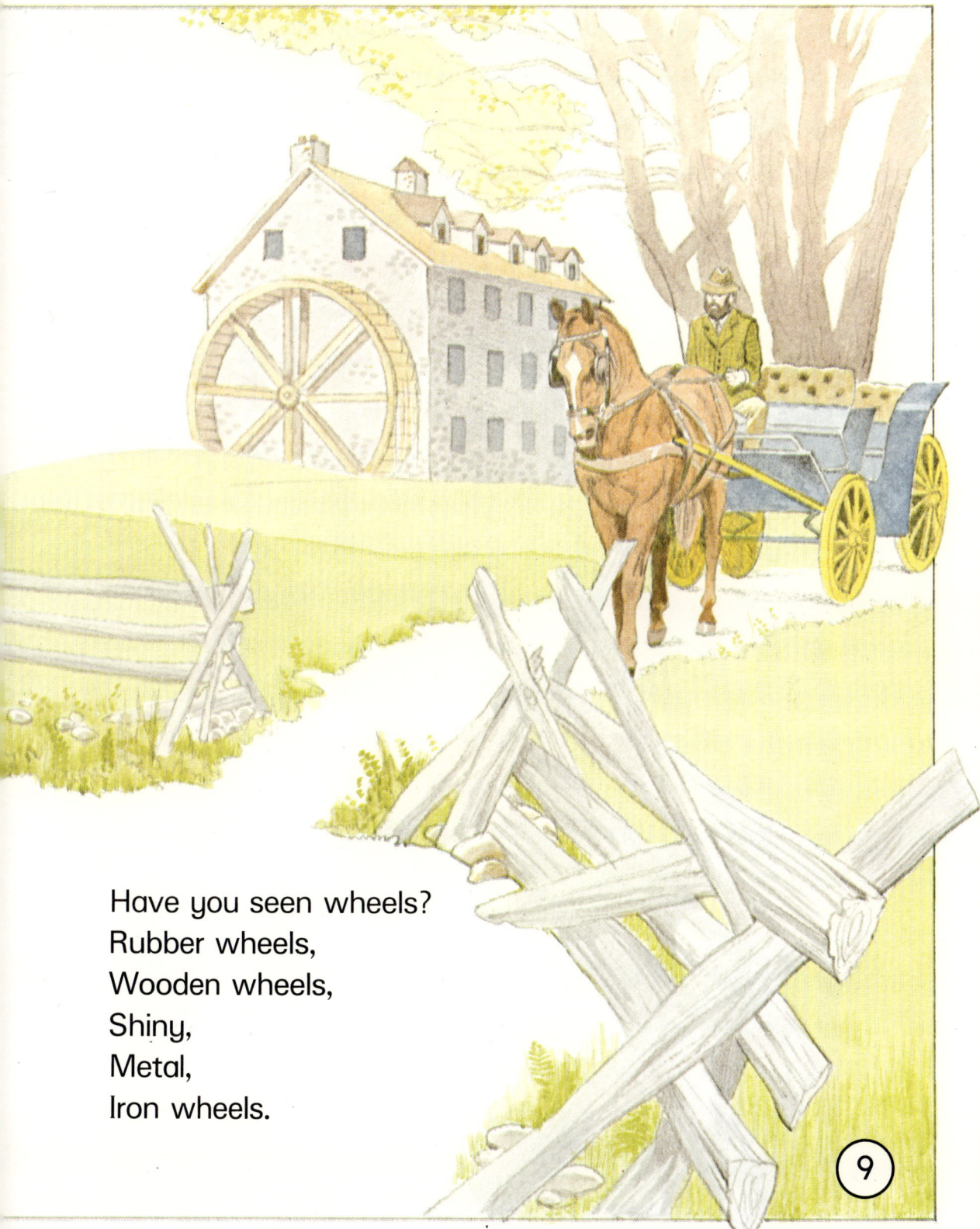

Have you seen wheels?
Rubber wheels,
Wooden wheels,
Shiny,
Metal,
Iron wheels.

9

Have you seen wheels?
Boats on wheels,
Bikes on wheels,
Trains on wheels,
Planes on wheels,
Cars,
Trucks,
Whizzing
Down the streets on wheels.

Have you seen wheels?
Wheels to sell a treat,
Wheels to clean a street,
Wheels to carry a load,
Wheels to build a road,
Fire-engines,
Police cars,
Zooming
Down the streets on wheels.

That's Good, That's Bad

By Christel Kleitsch
Illustrated by David Simpson

"There was a boy called Mark.
One morning he went for a ride in his go-kart."
"That's good."

"No, that's bad. One of the wheels fell off."
"Oh, that's bad."

"No, that's good. A man came by in a very old wagon."
"Oh, that's good."

"No, that's bad. The wagon got stuck in deep mud."
"That's bad."

"No, that's good. There was a bike
in the wagon."

"That's good."

"No, that's bad. The bike got
a flat tyre."

"That's bad."

"No, that's good. There was
someone selling skateboards."

"Oh, that's good."

"No, that's bad.
There was not one left."
"That's bad."

"No, that's good. A bus stopped to pick Mark up."
"That's good."
"No, that's bad. The hill was too steep for the bus."
"That's bad."

"No, that's good. Mark's mother came along in her car."
"Oh, that's good."
"Yes, that's good. Mark was **very** tired!"

No Room

By Marilyn Souther

Illustrated by Deborah Drew-Brook-Cormack

It was a cold, grey day. An elephant
was walking to town. He was very wet.
Just then the elephant saw a bus.

"If I get on that bus, I'll be warm and dry,"
thought the elephant.

The bus stopped, and the elephant got on.

Then a giraffe saw the bus. She was
very cold and wet.

"If I get on that bus, I'll be warm and dry,"
the giraffe thought. The bus came to a stop.

"There's no room," said the elephant.

"I'm so cold," said the giraffe.

"Well, maybe I could make a little room for you,"
said the elephant.

The giraffe got into the bus. Now there was
a little room left in the bus.

Then a hippopotamus saw the bus.
He was very cold and wet.

"If I get on that bus, I'll be warm and dry,"
he thought. The bus came to a stop.

"There's no room," said the giraffe.

"I'm so wet," said the hippopotamus.

"Well, maybe we could find a little room
for you," said the giraffe.

"That's the last one," said the elephant.

The hippopotamus got into the bus.
Now there was very little room in the bus.

Then a kangaroo and her baby saw the bus.
The mother was very cold and wet.

"If we get on that bus, we'll be warm and dry,"
said the kangaroo to her baby. The bus came to a stop.

"There's no room," said the hippopotamus.

"I'm so cold," said the mother kangaroo.

"Oh, well," said the giraffe. "We'll make room."

"That's the **very** last one," said the elephant.

The kangaroo and her baby squeezed
into the bus. Now there was **no** room in the bus.

Then a little wet fly saw the bus.

"If I get on that bus, I'll be warm and dry," thought the fly. So in he went.

Well, there was room on the bus for the elephant. There was a little room for the giraffe and the hippopotamus. The kangaroo and her baby just squeezed in.

But that was all the bus could take.

CRASH! SMASH! The bus fell to bits.
The elephant sat on the wet street.
He looked at the giraffe.
The giraffe looked at the hippopotamus.
The hippopotamus looked at the kangaroos.
Then they all looked at the little fly.
    "I have to go now," said the fly.
And off he went as fast as he could.

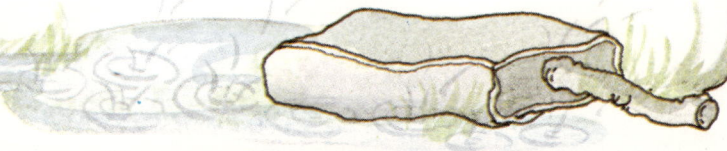

I Have a New Bike

By Gail Heald-Taylor
Illustrated by Lisa Smith

I have a new bike.
It has brand-new handlebars.
I have a new bike.
It has just two wheels.
I have a new bike.
It has big black tyres.
I have a new bike.
It has a basket to put things in.
I have a new bike.
It has a bell that rings.
I have a new bike.
It has a light on it.
I have a new bike.
I **love** it!

Beeny's Bike

By Christel Kleitsch
Illustrated by Maureen Shaughnessy

BUMP

Watch it! Hold on tight!
Beeny was trying to ride her new bike.
She went up her street to the top of the hill.
Then she started down. Faster, faster, and faster
she went. At the end of the hill, the bike hit a
bump.
CRASH!

Down went the bike and down went Beeny.
"Ow!" said Beeny. She kicked the bike
and it rolled away. It rolled along the street
and around the corner. Then it was gone.
"Good!" said Beeny.

Down the street it rolled. It rolled
right into Mrs. Bernardo. Bump went the bike.
Mrs. Bernardo looked around. "What was that?"
she said. But the bike was gone.

The bike rolled on. Fritz was sleeping
on the footpath. The bike rolled right into him.
Bump went the bike.

Fritz looked around. "What was that?"
But the bike was gone.

The bike rolled on. Mr. Hall was painting.
The bike rolled right into him. Bump went the bike.
Mr. Hall looked around. "What was that?"
he said. But the bike was gone.

At last the bike stopped at Beeny's house.
"My bike is back," said Beeny. "I'm glad."
"Now I'll try to ride to the end
of the street."
And away went Beeny on her bike.

QUEEN STREET

HOPE STREET SCHOOL

HOPE STREET

CHUN·SING
FRUITS & VEGETABLES

OPEN

75p Each

89p LB

39p 100g.

1·59

LONG ROAD

QUEEN ST.

Where did Beeny's bike go?

29

First Day

By Christel Kleitsch
Illustrated by Muriel Wood

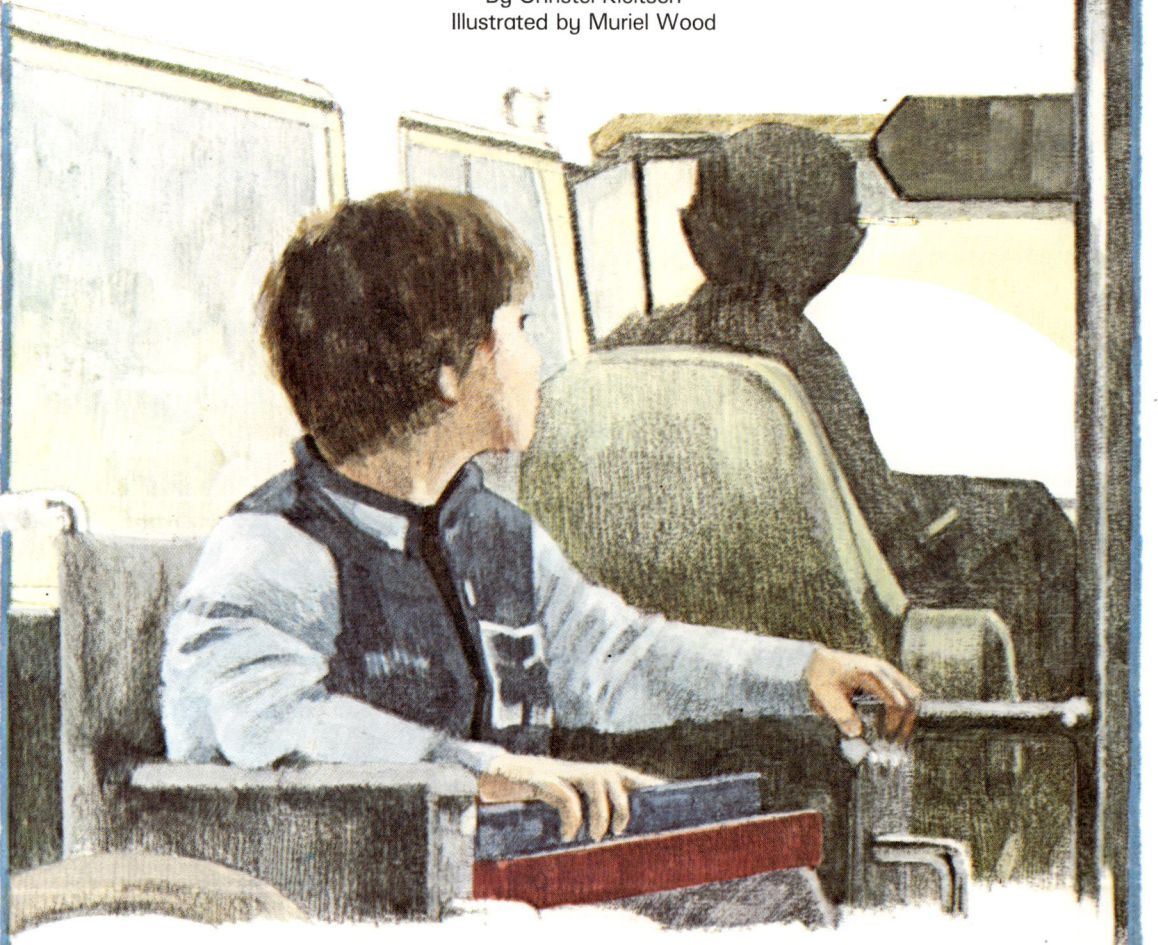

Going to school on a bus is fun. When I get on, my friend, Mrs. Mills, tells a joke. I watch the cars going by. I watch the kids walking to school. But today is my first day at my new school. I hope the kids will like me. I hope I like them.

At first the kids in my class just look at me.
Then they ask me about my wheelchair.
They ask about my leg braces and crutches, too.
    I tell them, "I ride in a wheelchair
because I can't walk. Sometimes I want to stand.
My braces and crutches help me stand.
Sometimes I need help. Sometimes I don't."

We have books here that we had in my old school. My desk is at the side of the class. The boy who sits beside me is Alex. I help him, and sometimes he helps me. Maybe we will become friends.

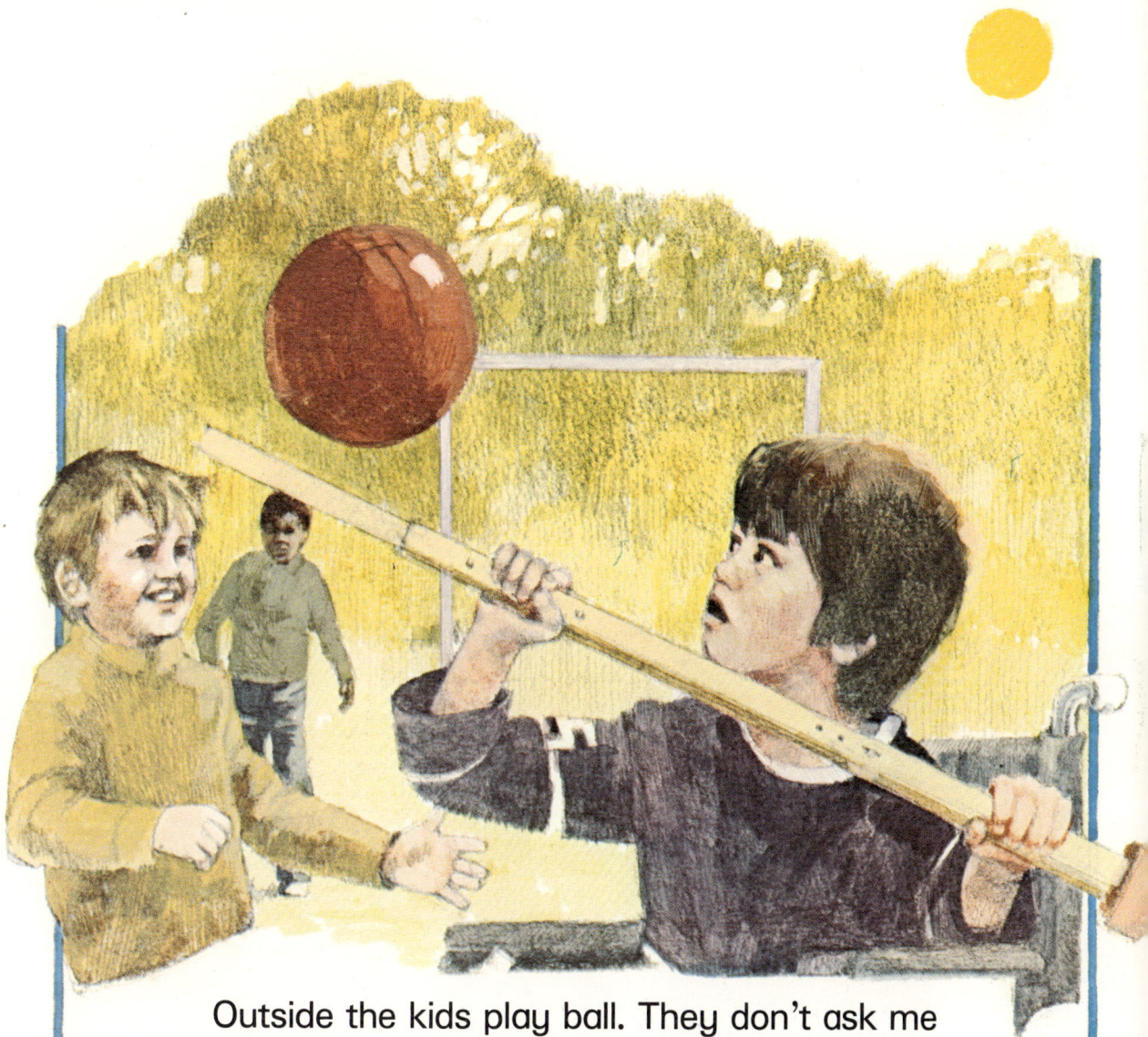

Outside the kids play ball. They don't ask me to play with them. Maybe they think I can't play because I can't walk. I just watch them play.

But when the ball comes to me, I hit it back with my head. I can hit the ball with my crutches, too. The kids see that I can play ball.

Then they ask me to play. I get a goal!
    Back in class, Alex and I find a book of jokes.
I look for a good one to trick Mrs. Mills.
I find one and tell it to Alex.
        "What would you do if your toe fell off?"
        "Call a tow truck."
(34)   Alex likes my joke.

When school is out, Alex comes with me
to the bus. Mrs. Mills likes my joke, too.
I ask Alex to tell one, but he's shy.
    At home my mum asks me how my first day was.
I say, "Just great!"

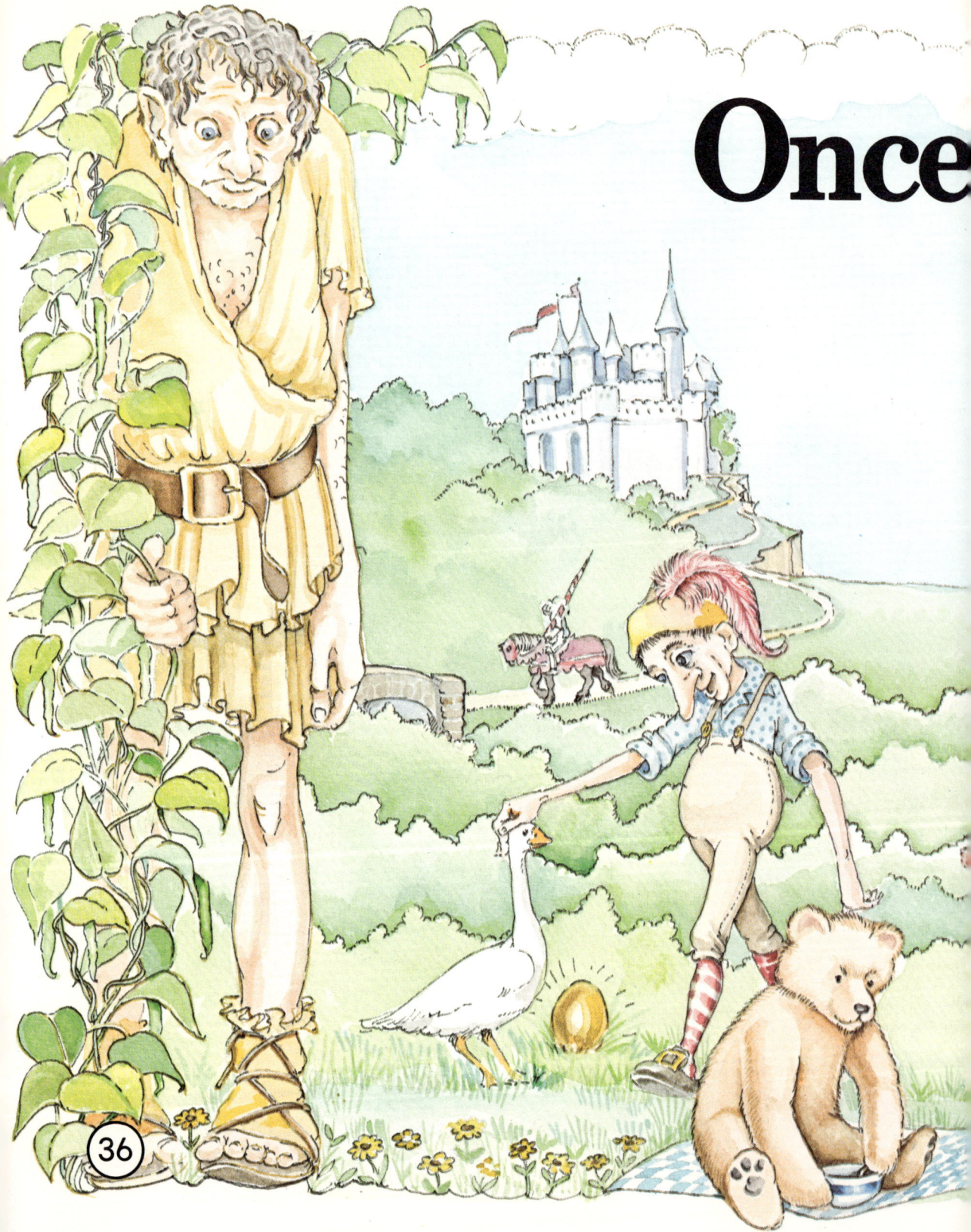

Once

Upon a Time

Once Upon a Time,
Once Upon a Time!
Everything that happened, happened
Once Upon a Time!

By Eleanor Farjeon

Once Upon A Time

by Kathleen Doyle
Illustrated by June Lawrason

I like a story that begins, "Once upon a time".
I like it because there are kings and queens and
princes.

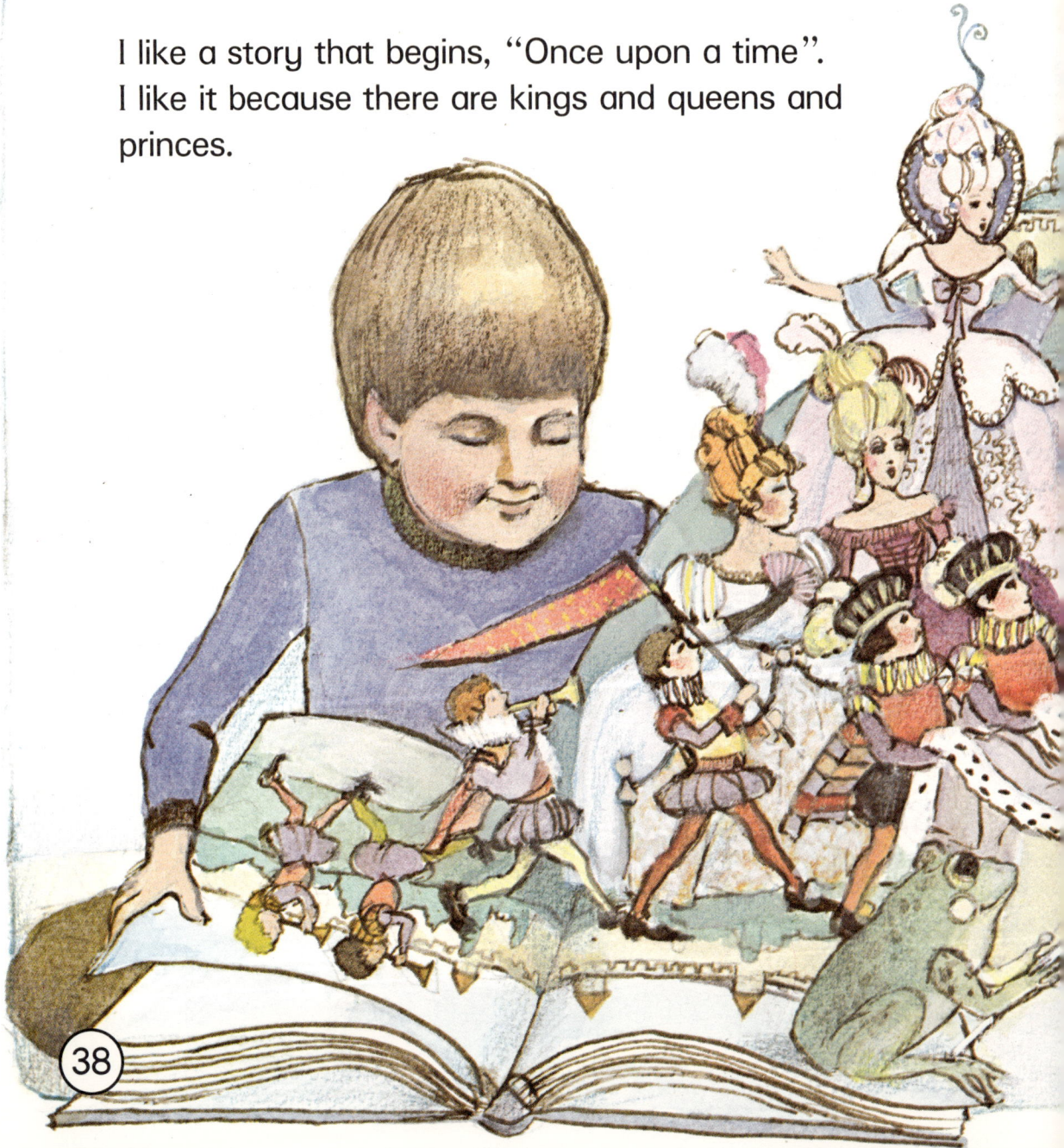

I like a story that begins, "Once upon a time".
I like it because there are frogs that become princes,
and because there are houses made of gold.

I like a story that begins, "Once upon a time".
I like it because there are giants as tall as a
house, and because there are houses
that have magic pots.

The Three Billy Goats Gruff

Illustrated by June Lawrason

Once upon a time, there were three billy goats who were called Gruff.

One day the Three Billy Goats Gruff saw that all the grass on the hill was gone. So they went to look for a new hill with new grass.

To get to a new hill, the Three Billy Goats Gruff had to go over a bridge. Now under this bridge lived a troll. He was mean, and he liked to eat billy goats.

Little Billy Goat Gruff went over the bridge first.
Trip, Trap! Trip, Trap! Trip, Trap!

"Who's that going over my bridge?" yelled the troll.
"I'm going to gobble you up!"

"Oh, please don't," said the Little Billy Goat.
"Big Billy Goat Gruff will be next. Eat him because
he's much bigger than I am."

"Well then, go on," said the troll.

Next Big Billy Goat Gruff went over the bridge.
TRIP, TRAP! TRIP, TRAP! TRIP, TRAP!

"Who's that going over my bridge?" yelled the troll.
"I'm going to gobble you up!"

"Oh, please don't," said the Big Billy Goat.
"Great Big Billy Goat Gruff will be next. Eat him because he's much bigger than I am."

"Well then, go on," said the troll.

Then Great Big Billy Goat Gruff went over the bridge.
TRIP, TRAP! TRIP, TRAP! TRIP, TRAP!

"Who's that going over my bridge?" yelled the troll.
"I'm going to gobble you up!"

"Oh, no you will not!" said the Great Big Billy Goat.
Great Big Billy Goat butted the troll with his
great big horns — right into the water.

And that was the end of the troll.

43

There Are Trolls

By John F. Green
Illustrated by Deborah Drew-Brook-Cormack

Trolls live in tree stumps
And live in old fridges.
There are trolls up the chimney
And some under bridges.

There are trolls that eat lemons
And some that eat snakes.
There's one (I've been told)
That gobbles up rakes.

The Enormous Turnip

Illustrated by Laurie McGaw

Once upon a time, an old man planted
a little turnip. He said to the little turnip,
"Grow, little turnip! Grow bigger and bigger!"
And the turnip did grow and **grow** and
GROW.

45

One day the old man thought, "This turnip is enormous. It's time to pull it up and eat it." So the old man pulled and pulled again, but he couldn't pull the turnip up.

He called the old woman to come and help. So the old woman pulled the old man, and the old man pulled the turnip. They pulled and pulled again, but they couldn't pull the turnip up.

Then the old woman called the dog.
He came out to help them. The dog pulled
the old woman, the old woman pulled the old man,
and the old man pulled the turnip. They pulled
and pulled again. Still they couldn't pull
the turnip up.

So the dog called the cat. She came out
to help them. The cat pulled the dog, the dog pulled
the old woman, the old woman pulled the old man,
and the old man pulled the turnip. They pulled
and pulled and pulled again. Still they couldn't pull
the turnip up.

Then the cat called the mouse. She came out
to help them. The mouse pulled the cat, the cat
pulled the dog, the dog pulled the old woman,
the old woman pulled the old man, and the old man
pulled the turnip. They pulled and they pulled
and they pulled again. And **up** came the turnip.

The turnip fell on the old man,
the old man fell on the old woman,
the old woman fell on the dog,
the dog fell on the cat,
and the cat fell on the mouse.
The poor little mouse was as flat as a pancake!
But they all had turnip to eat that night.

Chicken Forgets

Adapted from the book by Miska Miles
Re-illustrated by Marilyn Mets

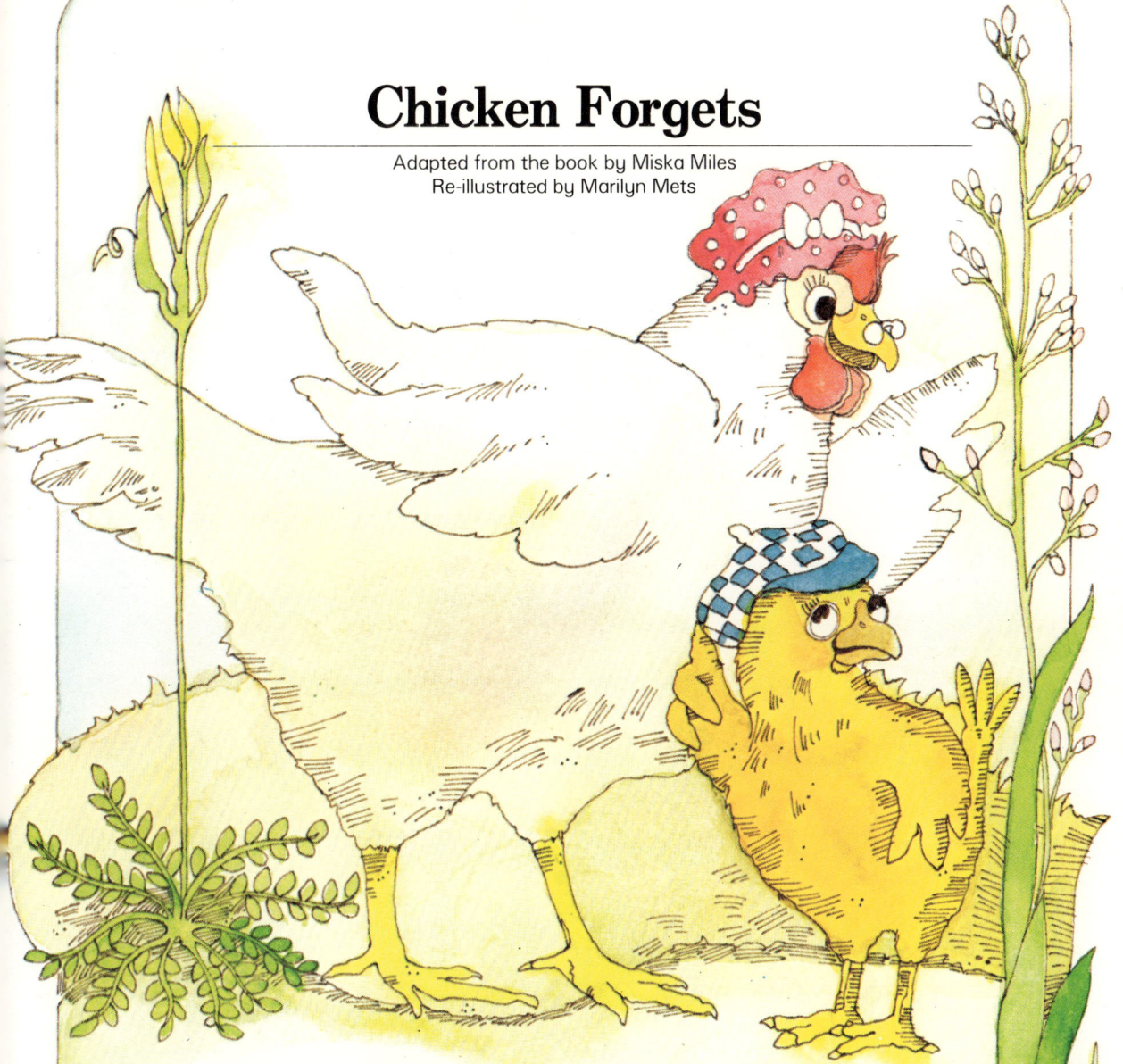

MOTHER HEN: Chicken, I need your help.
Would you go berry picking for me?
If you get a basket of blackberries,
I'll make a blackberry pie.

LITTLE CHICKEN: All right. I like to go berry picking.
MOTHER HEN: Take this basket and fill it
to the top. Sometimes you forget things.
This time, please, please think about
what you're doing. Please don't forget.
LITTLE CHICKEN: I won't forget, Mother. I'll get
some blackberries.

STORYTELLER: He started on his way. He didn't want
to forget, so he said over and over:
LITTLE CHICKEN: Get blackberries. Get blackberries.
STORYTELLER: All the way to the river he said:
LITTLE CHICKEN: Get blackberries.

STORYTELLER: Then the chicken saw an old frog.

FROG: What are you saying?

LITTLE CHICKEN: Get blackberries.

FROG: If you're talking to me,
you should not say that.

54

LITTLE CHICKEN:	What should I say?
FROG:	Get a big green fly.
STORYTELLER:	The chicken thought and thought. He didn't want to forget, so he started to say:
LITTLE CHICKEN:	Get a big green fly. Get a big green fly.
STORYTELLER:	All the way to the field he said:
LITTLE CHICKEN:	Get a big green fly.

STORYTELLER: At the field the chicken saw a goat.
GOAT: If you are talking to me,
you shouldn't say, "Get a green fly."
You should say, "Get green weeds."
LITTLE CHICKEN: Oh?
STORYTELLER: And the little chicken went on his way.
He started to say:
LITTLE CHICKEN: Get green weeds. Get green weeds.

RABBIT: No, no. Blackberries are best. I know
where you can get them. Come with me.

STORYTELLER: So the little chicken went with the rabbit.
He came to a big patch of blackberries.
The little chicken filled his basket
from the patch. Then he went home.
Back he went through the field. He ate
three blackberries. Back he went
by the river. And he ate
three more blackberries.

STORYTELLER: At home, the mother hen looked at the basket.

MOTHER HEN: You didn't forget. You have blackberries in the basket.

LITTLE CHICKEN: I told you I could do it!

MOTHER HEN: Good! Now I'll make you a blackberry pie.

Meet Beatrix Potter

By Lou Arrell
Illustrations by Beatrix Potter

Do you know this rabbit? His name is Peter.
You may know the story of Peter Rabbit.
Beatrix Potter thought of this story a long time ago.
Beatrix Potter didn't write *Peter Rabbit*
as a book. She first sent the story in a letter
to a little boy who was sick.

The letter began like this:
My dear Noel,
       I don't know what to write to you,
so I shall tell you a story about four little
rabbits . . .

The letter told the rest of the story. Do you know
the end of it?

Beatrix Potter had lots of animals for pets.
The pets she liked best were rabbits. Peter was one
of her pet rabbits. She made up a lot of books
about rabbits.

Another pet she had was a hedgehog named
Mrs. Tiggy-Winkle. This is what Mrs. Tiggy-Winkle
looked like in Beatrix Potter's book about her.
Mrs. Tiggy-Winkle liked to sleep a lot and drink tea
out of little cups.

Beatrix Potter made up funny names
for the animals in her books.
This duck is called Jemima Puddle-Duck.
Jemima lived on a farm and had to find
somewhere to lay her eggs.
She took a long trip to find
a good spot for her nest.

Beatrix Potter had pet mice who lived
in her house. She liked to watch them play.
Hunca-Munca was one of her mice.
Beatrix wrote a book about Hunca-Munca
and Tom Thumb. It was called
The Tale of Two Bad Mice. Can you see why?

Find some books by Beatrix Potter and look
at them. What other books do you like?

Journeys

Level Four
That's Good, That's Bad

ART DIRECTOR/DESIGNER
Hugh Michaelson

TYPESETTING
PFB Art & Type Ltd.

FILM
Colourgraph Reproduction Systems Inc.

PRINTING
Chorley & Pickersgill Ltd.